TUESDAY

Volume 8, 2014
Sandra Mason and Ruth F. Harrison,
eds.

Tuesday Writers constitute the oldest continuous writer group in Lincoln County, Oregon, founded by Ruth F. Harrison in 1990 on the heels of a course she offered at our community college. The group is notable for its literary fellowship and the success of various members over the years as they complete projects, publish books, and win awards. This past year witnessed new books of poems by members Ruth F. Harrison, *among the cat tales*, and by Sandra Mason, *Lost and Found*. Mason also took first place in the Dueling Judges category in the Oregon Poetry Association for "Sweeping: Three Scenes."

Tuesday members have come and gone, but Ruth continues to anchor our group after these twenty-three years, and members respect her as our literary *eminence grise*. The group has met every Tuesday (now Thursday) no matter what else is going on in the world; we met even on that fateful Tuesday of September 11, 2001. Participants have attended from along the entire Oregon seaboard, from Pacific City to the north to Florence to the south, and we have seasonal members from Colorado and Maine. It is a diverse group, hearing both poetry and prose—mostly essays and memoir stories—from participants. Each year we acknowledge and celebrate our work in this anthology, currently volume 8.

Current members of Tuesday include:

Ruth Harrison   Shirley Plummer
Sandra Mason   Kelly Mc Dowell
Marg Petersen

And on occasion

Kathleen Sullivan   Pat Ranzoni (from Maine)
Brian Hanna   Sue McGhee (from Colorado)

Contents

Ruth F. Harrison

Of that one talent	1
Future Perfect, Yet How Intense	2
Arcos: stones of the square	3
Milton's God	4
Conversation 1: woman and tree	6
Considering a "Comfortable Disease"	8
Watchers	9

Shirley Plummer

a haiku	10
Content	10
Grandma Travis' Pickle Barrel	11
The task of falling rain	12
Three Fibonacci poems:	
love follows, garden, three-toed sloth	13
By the Sea	14
To Find Peace	14
removing	15

Patricia Ranzoni

Eleven Hours Driving and Flying	
Portland to Portland	16
Come by	18
With	19
Next Spring, Or, If February wouldn't	
Pass	20

Sandra Mason

For the Poet Laureate of Bucksport, Maine
    upon the Loss of her Mother   21
You Again   22
A Mondo and a Kata-uta   23
The Teacher Grows Old   24
Taoist Toasts   25
Growing Old with Mother   26
Another Lullaby   32

Sue McGhee

Puma Skies: a novel (excerpt)   35

Brian Hanna

Theater of the Absurd   41

Kelly McDowell

There Were a Dozen or So   51
A Thought on Perspective   52
and so it goes   52
The Answer to the Question on
    Reincarnation   53
A Summer of Long Shadows (excerpt)   54

Marguerite K. A. Petersen

Widowed   61
Treasure   62
The Quiet Times   63

Authors

    64

Ruth F. Harrison

Of that one talent

I haven't any right to urge you on
when I have done so little with the gift,
hoarded it up for later use— such thrift!

Gifts stored are prone to mildew. One fine dawn
we'll find ourselves discarding quite a drift.
I haven't any right to urge you on
when I have done so little with the gift.

Then air it day by day, and practice long:
You'll undergo a high, a kind of shift
Of capability, a mental lift …

I haven't any right to urge you on
when I have done so little with the gift.
Hoarded it up for later use. What thrift.

--English madrigal, appeared
in *Poetry Depth Quarterly* , spring,
2005

Ruth F. Harrison

Future Perfect, Yet How Intense

We shall have arrived in the future
at 9:23.
The flight may have been perceived as
stimulating, the landing as silken
the limo and rental car timetables
as eclectic--
We shall have been surrounded by it-- all of it--
for eight minutes by 9:31.

All, all will have assembled there, the helipads
and jet-buggies, the air skis and cellophane
wings, the lucite zithers and gamelans
areaways lined with buckets of cosmos,
tubs of moonflower ...
For the occasion we shall have pierced our lips, be
wearing studs of chrysoprase
shall have plaited one tiny fashionable braid in
our upright hair;
designers
will have tied our hemline about one knee

Every person will have been happy for an hour and
25 seconds.

Women, men will have been
drinking cherry espressos, dipping
chamomile hips in whipped brandy, the
hors d'oeuvres ordered in serried rows, oh,
and
there will have been laughing and singing and
flashing of teeth, and
the outer darkness will have been declared a
mistake, will have been abolished by

unrescindable decree
and Lucifer blessed and forgiven, the
fallen angels redeemed

and reason and truth will have been seen to prevail
by 11:02 ....

--published in *Mind in Motion*, 1997

Ruth. F. Harrison

Arcos: stones of the square

Hawks cross and recross
the deeps below us. Various
people sitting. One, an old man,
perches on piled brownish slabs
of stone, a fence to mark
the boundary pause
between the placid plaza
and the deep. Olive groves, grayed
green, color the afternoon distances.
Spain's limpid sunlight wavers
on far fields of sunflowers
  a yellow mist
   the dust

--appeared in *Brevities*, Summer, 2007

Ruth F. Harrison

Milton's God

... and justify the ways of God to man.
--John Milton, *Paradise Lost*

... but I meant it for the best, God said. All I
did was, I only
told Adam I planned to repopulate Heaven
    with his kids. Little white lie.
Told him he'd live in Paradise and rule forever. Hell, it
was plausible—I'd lost one-third of the Heavenly Host
        when Lucifer got big-headed. Everybody
            knew that. All Adam had to do was

                What I
                    Say.

'Course I knew he wouldn't—what have I got omniscience
        for? I made him that way. Made
            Eve that way too.
Made the Tree, made Lucifer, knew he'd fall—man, I
    set up the whole thing.

I like games, see. And I'd got bored making stars and
        universes; I wanted somebody to play with.
    And Adam—he was such a dumb clown—he took me
        seriously. He thought I'd
        really do it—let him rule

in Paradise and live forever.
'Course he did. He had
to believe me, I was God.

Besides, when I said *eternal life*, what I
Really meant was—
It would seem like eternity.

--in *Mind in Motion,* Issue #43, 1997

Ruth F. Harrison

Conversation 1: woman and tree

A woman said to a tree you shine in the sun. Those
caterpillars eat your top leaves. Why don't you
just say no caterpillar teeth? A tree said we are
of the part of living beings whose task it is to be
eaten. A woman said but why why why? perfection

is beauty. You have a right to rebel. Would you be
happy a tree said if the wheat rebelled?

Well but well but said a woman well.

Wheat is beautiful too said a tree.

But in late summer a woman said your leaves will
have many caterpillar-teeth holes and your top
branches will be bare sticks. Yes said a tree.
My eyes will find it tedious looking at you said a
woman in summer with bare stick branches and holes
eaten in the leaf. What is tedious said a tree.

I mean right now my eyes gladden to see your clean
bright leaf and will be tired in summer by seeing
only sticks and holes. We should step on those
caterpillars step step step step step. What is step
said a tree.

Well said a woman you could make poison in your
leaves then or something. Are you some kind of
caterpillar doormat? A tree said what is doormat.
A doormat is something said a woman a person

walks on, going home.

Oh said a tree yes. I am a caterpillar doormat and
a bird doormat and an ant doormat. But why said a
woman why why why. The best part of my task said a
tree is to cradle some feet going home.

--in *Mind in Motion,* Issue #47, 1999

Ruth F. Harrison

Considering a 'Comfortable Disease'

Not going forward is, of course,
Dying in place, that much is clear. Yet

As I scuff this leaf, tread this duff, shelter
In honeyed air under these boughs

Old brain, lizard-happy, basks easy
And takes comfort in met needs.

Need shade, need bark smells, need
To see big, see green, look up to light

Need holy, need quiet rustling in fern fronds
Pitch scent, hush of wind on leaf, this breath ...

New brain, now, deplores pot-holes,
Admires smooth asphalt, a chrome-steel gleam

This now lacquered hairstyle, bright green lawn,
Tissues, prefaded denims, a stick-free pan ...

Fast lane's a surface pace, all very of course
Yet horsetail rises through two feet of tar—

Old brain asks: where water? Find roots ...
Where warning bird? Night-spirit bird? Where worms?

Perilous to muzzle her—that deep one will out
Being song's source, pusher of our heart's pulse

Muck-dweller, sluggard slow and wallowing, she is yet
Sole base connection to Old All-That-Is ...

-- in *Mind in Motion*, Issue #45, 1998

Ruth F. Harrison

Watchers

Wake, for the hour has come to throw off sleep;
Some small flame glimmers in our soul's dark night.
We watch and wait for light across the deep

and though it isn't easy yet, to keep
a darklong vigil for some phantom sight,
we wake. The hour has come to throw off sleep.

In the black reaches of the night, some weep
wanting a solid word, a hope more bright—
and watch and wait for light across the deep.

We browse our lives like flocks of well-fed sheep
moving from field to fold, not conscious, quite
Wake! for the hour has come to throw off sleep.

There will be time hereafter for such sleep
as follows battle. Set your spirit bright
to watch and wait for light across the deep.

Our lives are lent us briefly, not to keep;
our chance to learn to soar is small and slight.
Wake! for the hour has come to throw off sleep
to watch and wait for light across the deep.

--Appeared in *Pen &
Ink,* Spring/Summer, 1996

Shirley Plummer

glassy lake
smooth v-wake widens
a silent loon glides

--published on-line, *cattails* ed. 2, May 2014, haiku, p. 10

Content

The sight of a man with bare legs and sandaled feet, protected by a straw cape and pointed straw hat from the heavy slanting rain, was commonplace to Basho but is picturesque to me. Why can I not be satisfied with what is common here and now? A bicyclist on highway 101 would have to hide from this wind; but, he might be out in heavy rain...

envy in sun
pity in wind and rain –
bedraggled cat

--published on-line, *cattails* ed. 3, Sept. 2014, haibun, p.15

Shirley Plummer

Grandma Travis' Pickle Barrel

Each year she made a barrel of dill pickles
meant to last through the winter for her large family
It sat in the cellar keeping cold

One of mother's earliest childhood memories
her first chore --- going down the dark, damp steps
every evening to fetch pickles up for supper

removing rock and plate that held them down
away from the air, barehanded pulling out pickles
scurrying up out of the cold to the warmth of the kitchen

As winter progressed she stood on tiptoe
to reach deeper into the barrel
taking longer each day to capture enough

By spring she was rolling her sleeve
up onto her shoulder, putting her
entire arm into the cold brine

fishing for the last pickles
hoping to find enough for everyone
and trying not to fall in

Shirley Plummer

the task of falling rain

to lay dust
and wash leaves
to brighten blossoms
and make the earth smell new
to cool a summer day
and make a casual walk pleasant
to play a tune on the shimmering leaves
a lullaby on a tent, a tattoo on a skylight

to allow one to feel again like a small child --
tongue tasting rain -- jumping on puddles

to mask and wash away gentle tears for
long ago remembrances

Shirley Plummer

Three Fibonacci poems

love follows   (letters)

o
to
the
end of
the earth
my love follows:
where your whim leads I go

garden   (syllables)

I
arrange
my garden
pulling less-liked plants
and those least happy in their place
allowing almost all but the too obstreperous.
So, I edit my garden for variety, balance, beauty and
             serenity.

three-toed sloth (words)

An
ai foot
has three toes
each with a long claw
curved like a clothes hanger over a branch
Hanging beneath by its twelve toes the animal moves
       slowly, hand over hand
so to speak; its motion is visible because of its large size,
     and because it is speedier than a banana slug

Shirley Plummer

By the Sea

An hour of fading light remains
of this summer night, and the sweetbriar,
the eglantine of Shakespeare,
has furled its flowers

These long, light evenings pay
reparations for short, dark days
that make us wish to den with the bears
wild storms blow danger

To Find Peace

Each day I watch the sea

One diminishing wave
slides back under the next
draws me with it
out to sea
to the center of light and water

Unsure of myself
out or in
or dissolved in the expanse
I stand looking ---
seeking serenity

Shirley Plummer

Removing

reluctant to move yet again
even to escape the bone-chilling damp cold
preserved from thinking often of moving
by the sneak faux summer days
scattered throughout the winter
like broken sunlight glittering on the sea

Patricia Ranzoni

Eleven Hours Driving and Flying
Portland to Portland

and then some, leaving Carol grieving her frostbit tomatoes
covered in vain. May's last full moon fulfilling its
reputation
in Maine.

From the air we can see earth's greening, coast to coast,
even at night, migrating with untold flocks across their
flyways.
One need only sense and believe. Easy feel above it all,
life on earth, winging with unknowable hosts gone, too,
from home, circling our particular globe, praying to touch it
again.

When white Mt. Hood appears in the plane window,
perfect,
majestic through the dark, it feels like God. Hard to
believe.

Carol will set out more flats for her winter store because
winter will
return, God, a blizzard through the panes. But not before

hemispheres
release another year's beings, whether beloved or despised, in all
the ways they will rise.

Our seat mate with seizure worries, her service dog tucked under
the scrimmed-off first-class rear in front of us next to our
carry-ons
with our own aides, makes every hard-to-grasp aura
believable.
Mt. Hood, for example. Buddy, rescued and trained.
Carol's hands
in the soil over the ledge back home, last winter's saved
egg shells,
crumbled, edging each bed and seedling reaching for life.

Believe what you will. We all have to.

Patricia Ranzoni

Come By

lament for the summer of 2014

I'll put the tea on but I should warn you I might wail.

Our son is suffering from a distracted driver turning into
his cycle's commuting route without stopping at the sign,
his crushed and sheared shoulder and arm bones grafted,
plated, and screwed together for as long as 13 pins hold,
his life's work heaving stone done.

And our beloved boys, Ismail, Zakaria, Ahed, and
Mohamed,
9, 10, and 11, buried in the sand where they were shot
playing ball on that ghetto shore by occupying boat
gunners.

And you no doubt heard about whole schools of our girls
disappeared for being girls. And our innocent little ones
thrown into sexual exploitation, hard labor, begging, and
war
around the world. Fresh rose geranium leaves or mint?

Ginger for the nausea. For the sickening hatred spewing
at the border for our thousands of children fleeing their
America, falling off train tops, dying in the desert.
Violated, terrorized. Fear beyond fear and unending shame
come by....

> But all I have to offer
> is my darkest-grained bread
> and this Olive Honey Spread
> from the Palestinian Fair Trade farmers.

Fair.

Come by. We'll take tea to the wellhouse
but beware -- I might wail.

With

if you can't see me beside you

it's because I am right behind you

standing back

from the flames of your grief

if you should turn to me

I am here   tending the old fire

our mothers are burning into us

From *Leavings* (Bay River Press, 2005)

Patricia Ranzoni

Next Spring, Or,
If February wouldn't pass,

we could pretend you haven't gone.
That the phone will bring your sound soon.

If we don't finish Christmas, leaving
the string of cards over the arch,
their cardinals won't have flown either
nor their snowmen sunk.

If we don't exchange last gifts,
the few we could do this time,
don't toast with the brandied pear,
Christmas and you might still be here. No?

If the red of hearts could stay, the tier
of Valentine sweets, and the miniature potted rose,
could February stay *would you?*

But the plant's shiny-red wrap
spreads wings as if readying to go,
reflective of your long lift.

If February just wouldn't pass. . . .

but the raccoons and minks
wouldn't be courting through the snow,
coyotes and foxes singing their love,
sap rising in everything live.

> *You, not off*
> *becoming your own next Spring.*

Sandra Mason

For the Poet Laureate of Bucksport, Maine upon the Loss of her Mother

In April, think of seeds.
Walk again the favorite meadow path.
Let your eye relearn the news of green
in tiny neon filaments
that strive once more to life.

August wafts over your senses
with plenty, vines adroop
with winter provision.
She would have thought harvest,
blanching, canning, Mason jars a-row on the sill.

November forecasts a hunkering-down,
logs stacked like sentinels
of protection, defense. How high
this season's snow? The soft
whiteness of its January cloak

like her mantle of glorious hair
drying gently in the flickering warmth,
sign of wisdom, sign of nurturance,
shield against the sorrow
of seasons that pass in silence.

Sandra Mason

You Again

In your last two pictures
something derelict, maybe desperate.
Who would share a photo like this?
Bloated face, swollen eyes,
a look so flushed it's feverish,
that no-pain grin—
always with arms around
a stranger unnamed.

Is something wrong with your eyes?
It's the beard, you say.
Is something *wrong* with your eyes?

What does the universe demand?
You want to mess up the molecules
of your soul . . . in which
you do not believe.
You want no trace of having been.
It shows.

Something has mugged you and stolen
your heart. You're a changeling now.
Trolls pilfered your elan vital
and left a good-time zombie.

You are moorless. Your path is no-path,
the feel-good way you see as rebellion.

You want no change.

I want . . .

another photograph.
A different cast of characters.
That old face.
You, again.

A Mondo and a Kata-uta

Why cobwebs dangling from the ceiling?
Spring cleaning unclutters my mind.

Does the hummingbird rest?
Waves of red striped petunias
overflow the planter.

Sandra Mason

The Teacher Grows Old

Draw a blueprint based on
all words have built before,
Acropolis, Cheops, Pisa,
Chichen Itza, igloo of ice.

Take imagination by the hand
and walk through these bones:
here is your study, here your nursery,
here the hearth supplying daily warmth.

Leave interning architects alone to stew—
what turret to be devised, what whimsical roof,
what gingerbread to embellish?
Return and see collapse of the house of hope.

Like women of Wurzburg, guardians of abode,
sort through rubble plank by board. Amass piles
of like, unlike. Recommend three-penny nails.
Lay the foundation again and close your eyes.

To shelter you in doddery, it rises, magnificent
house of the mind, Khan's Xanadu,
Odysseus' branching tree-bed, strong,
known by Penelope magical and true at last.

Sandra Mason

Taoist Toasts

Here's to the space contained within the walls of the vessel!

Hipahipa to the unnamed and unnamable mother of everything!

Lechaim to truth abiding behind the finger which points at the moon!

Nazdorovya to our teachers, vacant like valleys, dull like muddy waters!

Prost to the wood waiting to be fashioned into function!

Skol to the spirit that surrounds us as the ocean enfolds its fish!

Salud to a person walking on a path!

Kong chien to one who reaches for a strawberry while dangling between two tigers!

Cin cin to the simplicity of water!

Kampai to being here now!

Sandra Mason

Growing Old with Mother

My mother is wearing a ring none of her daughters has ever seen before on the finger where her diamond wedding set used to be a permanent fixture. It's a gaudy and cheap-looking affair, pink and red stones set in swirls of a base metal. When we ask her about it, she says, "Oh, I've been wearing this a long time," but we know it appeared only yesterday.

This is the second time in three years her wedding set has been "lost" in the memory care unit at the home. The first time the staff undertook an investigation that went on for weeks. They and we moved all the furniture and looked everywhere, in drawers, in and under the bed, in the folds of chairs, under the chairs, over and over. Suddenly, after I told them it was time to bring in the police, the rings reappeared under her chair—where everyone had looked a dozen times. This time her rings reappeared in one of her drawers—but no one has accounted for the strange ring she's wearing in exchange. We've decided to let her keep wearing the imitation replacement and store her wedding set safely elsewhere. Dad bought her this expensive set decades after they were married, when he felt more prosperous, to replace her simple gold band, which had been all he could afford when they first married in 1940 in a South Dakota caught in the edge of the Dust Bowl. Once she began wearing the set, she never removed it.

Mom is remarkable for her staunch Protestant prairie values and her undaunted work ethic. She has never been too dainty or too feminine to pitch in and get a job done. Duty comes to her without a second thought. Once, when a relative remarked on Mom's "uprightness," we naturally thought she meant strong moral character, but she was actually referring to her good posture. I guess the two go well together. When I was a teenager, I recall Mom sitting down at the phone in an otherwise busy day of mothering **and** working downtown to make "her calls." As a member of the United Methodist Women, she checked in weekly on what was then called shut-ins, women who still lived in their own homes but who were ill or incapacitated and could no longer get out and about.

Now I suppose Mom—at 94—is the modern equivalent, someone whom you must visit in a room down a hall behind a door with a lock-code. She landed there after taking a long hike down busy Lancaster Drive with her walker and telling no one she was leaving. After turning left and right, she got tired and sat down. The home's van cruised the streets until they spotted her, and then they moved her behind the no-wander door.

Although Mom's daughters are approaching the genius category, their smarts come from Dad, who died more than thirty-five years ago. Her own mother suffered from osteoporosis and became ever smaller and shorter, rather stooped, in her 80s. Recently Mom's shoulders have become hunched, but she is sturdy and moves well, with her walker for balance. Grandma, I think, tipped the scales at barely 100 pounds; Mom holds in at a good 150. I suppose we should have noticed the progressive dwindling of her mental acuity. In her 70s she would ask to have very simple things explained to her, over and over again. If she started telling a story and you said you'd heard it already, she'd say, "Oh, well, anyway . . ." and continue in exactly the same words as before, as if once the needle were dropped on the record, the song had to proceed. The incapacitation is a gradual process, and as with the proverbial frog sitting in a pot of water coming slowly to the boil, we simply accommodated without remark.

Into her 70s she still marshaled her volunteer activities, driving around her more elderly friends, putting out rummage for the sale at church, managing to staff and supervise lunch at the senior center on Thursdays. It was the daunting thought of having to rake fallen leaves another time that convinced her at 80 to move into the retirement home, where originally she had her own small apartment. After she opened her apartment door to a knock, wearing nothing below her waist, the retirement staff indicated the need for assisted living, and then the long unsupervised walk a couple of years later placed her in memory care.

It seems that her cerebral decline disconcerts Mom herself less and less. She is visibly frustrated when she cannot find a word. She knows her daughters but maybe cannot recall their names and introduces them as her sister or her husband—but she seems very happy to see us. She calls the staff at the home "those relatives who live here." She can no longer focus on a TV show, nor can she sustain her attention to read or write. She religiously attends group events and enjoys live singers, puzzles, and bingo. She likes to thumb through books or magazines with photographs, and sometimes she talks about events years ago as if they were now. She often tells us she must get her coat so we can walk to the barn, or go see her mother (who died in the '80s) laid out at the funeral home, or that Dad and Grandpa (both long gone) will be home soon.

If we visit, by the next day she has forgotten. If we take her to a family holiday dinner, she seems overwhelmed, falls asleep in a chair, and by the next day does not recall anyone who was there, including herself. She has forgotten the names and relationship of her grandchildren. A couple of years ago we simply removed her telephone. If she got a wrong number, she took it seriously as if the call had been for her. If we called, she could not hear well enough to carry on a conversation; I'm sure it frustrated her as much as it did us.

This entire process has, I think, been harder on those who love her and knew her as she used to be. In small increments we have lost her, and we have individually grieved at every stage. I love going to see her; my heart leaps when her face lights up with recognition. We have nothing to talk about, as she can connect nothing with nothing. She has not a wrinkle on her rosy face, and she sports a pixie-ish haircut. Within all that has been lost, it seems as if her character shines forth even more clearly. She is like a sculpture of bones, over time polished and clarified to an intense sharpness and whiteness.

In her face I see the mother who taught me how to be a woman with my own inner strength—the moments she spent reading to me or working with me in the kitchen or helping me to sew. I think of the model she set for her daughters, just going about her work and doing what she needed to do. I think of her coming across the continent when she was 67 and re-learning to manage a stick shift in the snow to help me out when I'd had surgery and was forbidden to drive. I think of the times we did yard work together or the times we played hooky and just went for a drive through the valley to a tulip farm, all red and yellow stripes against the blue sky, or up the foothills of Mt. Hood to a hidden lake. I see now the beauty of those times was in the moment itself, as her memory of them is gone.

I think of her bravery in facing breast cancer and forging on through months of chemotherapy and years of Tamoxifen, which somehow she arranged to buy inexpensively through a friend who made trips to Mexico for that purpose. I think of her non-judgmental acceptance of just about everybody, including black sheep and late bloomers. I remember when, with me, her middle-aged baby, she was changing a fitted sheet and raced with me to get her corner done first— and then we giggled—for her, a rare moment of whimsical behavior.

I am relieved that she is safe, secure, clean, and well-tended. Many who work at the home adore her, as she is unfailingly cheerful and polite. We walked in one day to find a strange young woman in a uniform, a nurse's assistant, sitting on the floor with her head in Mother's lap. Funny, we thought, since Mom has never been much of a toucher or hugger. Mom seemed calm but rather nonplussed by this. She's everybody's image of a nice grandmother.

Another day a nurse asked her, "How do you feel?"

"About what?" Mom smilingly replied.

The same nurse asked her, "Would you like to go into the bathroom?"

Mom said, "Well, sure, I'll go in there with you if you want."

It soothes me to see her untroubled and secure and mostly without pain or discomfort. She is the living embodiment of the miracle that constructs every human in existence, biology and soul, and of the poignancy that attends mortality. As we sit together companionably, I am making do with just being there with her, in those moments that we have. We may have few of them left, and I miss her already.*

*Mildred Leota Olson Klein died on September 10, 2014 at age 94.

Sandra Mason

Another Lullaby

We sit in her room, too warm,
the unwatched TV
with a classic soccer game
replayed from years past,
the commentator screaming
en español.

Daddy had loved to watch golf.

These words are to her
like a snatch from a song she used to know,
a movement of color in the corner,
a companion,
one of the charmed and magical
things that surround her now.

Under pixie hair she's studded
with scattered pins,
her seamless cherub's face,
eyes at ease taking in all events
like the Buddha in a trance.
I think I see these images from her mind
floating between us, nothing
bridging a gap to connect,
words no longer bearing
the names of things.
She sees just beyond the words.
I want to study this language.

She tells me she has a machine.
You enter and say
where you want to go
and it will take you there.

I'd like one of those, I reply.
She smiles with what seems heavenly understanding,
indulging my earth-bound mind, my inadequate sense.
She went downtown in her machine.
She went to New York City.
She went to floors at the home that do not exist—
she calls them *places you don't know about*,
and I see that's where she really lives.

It makes a sudden sense to my stretching mind:

she wanders the halls trying to set things right,

to tell the police the facts about human injustice

to get the baby back to its mother
to inform the workers
she calls *those relatives who live here*
and take care of me
when the world is out of whack.

Half-written letters
with strangely-addressed envelopes
litter the counter, stamps
glued on willy-nilly.
She has wisdom to impart
to a mysterious correspondent.
This knowledge makes her uneasy.
She has work still to do.

Yet when she gazes at me
I know that light of kinship and yes,
of happiness. Does she see
her daughter? Can she teach
me the ABC's again, this time
of all I have yet to learn?
She has called me her sister,
my husband her husband,
and I am filled in my atoms with pride.

I am fiercely proud,
proud to know her unerringly kind spirit
her life an open testament to doing right
doing what's right
for a shut-in, a nephew dying of AIDs
a snake pestered by a cat
a hobo at the kitchen door.
These deeds and a lifetime of small wonders
one by one flitter in pastiche
across that face,
her serene and empty face,
like the handwriting on the wall,
and she tells me once more,
I am trying to get back home.

Sue McGhee

Puma Skies
a novel

Bernadette

I live in an adobe house in Bolivia and it is raining. In the southern hemisphere, April signals the onset of winter and dryer weather but here in the valley, it is raining. My coca bush had to be moved inside temporarily in order to save its leaves; it is a resilient plant but I don't like to take chances with it because coca is a staple in my medicine bag and I want to keep a fresh supply of leaves at all times. Catalina brought it in for me and set it next to my stove. And now she sits and studies her books while I strain to see Mount Tunari from the little window over the sink.

Cochabamba is a small town in the lowlands, with abundant fruit orchards, whose ripe smells fly the night winds and reach the upstairs rooms of fancy homes in Cala Cala, where children sleep safe and snug in little beds with embroidered covers and where the food is good and plentiful. I can't see much of the city from here, but I can sometimes hear student rumblings from the university yard – youngsters who are dissatisfied with one thing or another, but more than anything else – their government. Now, though, it is relatively calm and that is good because it is easier for me to get around and not worry about road blocks.

Today has been an exhausting day tramping through the mud as my car broke down once again. Dad keeps saying he will buy me a new car, but I tell him I am fine without one, though that is not true. He worries about me since we live so far apart, but I worry about him, too and his health. We two are all that's left now. Still, I will have to buy a new car soon; the old Renault has served me well over twenty years, since before Catalina was born and she is twenty four, but the repairs are costly and to replace parts is difficult as most are no longer available.

Catalina is my god child. I delivered her in this very house, all those years back, with Olympia looking on, sipping her brandy and soothing Francisca who was always my favorite. I turned the head and received the child in my hands, cut the cord and handed the baby to her mother. After she was washed and wrapped, Olympia pierced the baby's ears, cleanly and expertly and went back to her brandy.

Catalina was my first delivery but since then there have been many more, here and all around the Cordilleras: Felipé from Francisca's village up north near Trinidad, Carlita from Sucré and Maria, whose mother lived in an apartment building called Vino Tinto in LaPaz. Then there was the little girl I delivered near Los Niños up past Oruru. They wanted me to name her and I chose *Norwelia* for my best friend back in the old days, before the assassinations, before Nicky and his Vietnam, before Deer – long before Saint Ernesto.

I am tired now and Catalina has prepared me a cup of maté to ease the fatigue. She appraises me to see how long she must wait before she asks for some help with her books, but she knows it is best to let me rest. She is smart but her English is still not good and that is my fault, as we mostly speak to each other in Spanish.

The guinea pigs chirp their hunger from their nest beneath the stove; it is like a lullaby to me and I can't help dreading the day when they become dinner for a special occasion. Catalina surprises me with her zest for butchering them. It is her way as it was her mother's way, but Francisca made sure I was out of the house before she did it; she was a gentle soul and was sympathetic to my feelings. Her daughter is not as sensitive and I remember the pain on Deer's face when he saw how it distressed me.

Deer arrived after Nicky left and Ray had returned to the States to set up his medical practice. That was 1968 and I am feeling the weight of the past today more than most. I think that I am lonely, and I don't like to think that. I am, though. I am lonely.

* * * * * * * * * *

Jeremy

Jeremy's hands shook a bit as he waved goodbye to the little brown-eyed receptionist, then waited for her to smile before shuffling through the door of the office.

He liked this doctor. He seemed about the right age, having practiced for twenty years, yet not too old to embrace a new idea now and then, though he did seem a little dubious when he told him about Bernie. He knew he talked too much these days, bragging about her and her views on his medical care. He was proud of her, even though he had to endure her lectures, though a lot of what she said was true. She kept telling him how we've become a pill-popping society and that most doctors today treat the symptoms and not the cause and on and on she'd go. Western medicine is not helping you, Dad, she'd say, it's making you dependent on prescription after prescription and then another prescription to counter the effects of the others. Geez, the sermons he'd heard. She wanted to know what doctors he was seeing, why and what they were prescribing, how much exercise he was getting, how much beer he was drinking. But he knew it was for his own good. Funny, how the child eventually becomes the parent.

He had even shared some of her opinions with the good doctor today, his first visit with this guy, and they had both laughed. He showed him her picture and smiled and the doctor patted him on the back. She's lovely, he said. She was, too, especially after all she'd been through. She's quite a gal, Jeremy went on and the doctor agreed.

The doctor asked what kind of treatment he'd been on for his arthritis and Jeremy told him she wanted him to stay off the meds and walk more.

"Your daughter? Ok, but what about the pain?"

"She thinks the walking will ease the pain, Doc."

"Well, sometimes it does and sometimes it doesn't. What about you?" He peered over his glasses -- "cheaters," Bernie called them.

"She also says I need more Vitamin "C", more company and more laughter in my life. Like the guy who wrote that book, remember, years ago, back in the. . . I forget his name, but that guy who wrote about how laughter can cure you and proved it when he lay in a hospital with some kind of incurable disease and healed himself with old Marx Brothers' movies. . .? Remember?"

"Well, no not really. But yes," the doctor agreed, "a happy and fulfilling life can be very beneficial to your health, and pain can be managed in a smart and reasonable way without ill effects." He cleared his throat. "Then, I take it you're not on any pain medication?"

"Norman Cousins. That's who it was. Norman Cousins."

"Mr. McCallister?"

"Nothing. I don't take anything. But I try to laugh a lot." The doctor smiled sympathetically.

"Really!   Well, you've seen the deterioration of your lower back in these x-rays, Mr. McCallister.   You must be in quite a bit of pain."

"Right.   I know all about my spine from all the other doctors I've been too."

"And the pain?"

"I try to ignore it. Walking helps."

"I see."   A shadow of a frown flickered across the doctor's eyes.   "Well then, who is treating you?"

"You.   Maybe.   And Bernie. My daughter.   She keeps track of what I'm doing and who I'm seeing of course."

"Well of course, she's your daughter."

"But it's hard because of how far apart we are. She's down there with the natives most of the time, traveling with the Kallawaya, sometimes she's even in the jungle – they call it the "Green Hell" down there, you know, but it's the Amazon just the same, only not in Brazil. Sometimes she's gone for weeks without communication, no phone, no computer.   She loves it though.   Always did. We lived there for years while I was building roads.   She spent a lot of time trying to organize the natives as a kid, ditching school, riling the servants, making herself a nuisance with the cook, even though they ended up being good friends.   Her mother worried about her all the time, afraid she'd get kidnapped or . . ."

"Mr. McCallister, am I to understand that your daughter is your primary care physician?"

"Oh, no, Doc, she's not a physician. She's a shaman."

". . . a shaman." The doctor turned away and placed his cheaters atop his head. There was a long moment of silence. "Mr. McCallister, Sir. With due respect. How am I to treat you when I feel I'm to be monitored by your daughter living in a foreign country and who, again respectfully, sir, is not even a physician."

"I know, I know. It's awkward. But we don't have to tell her everything, Doc."

Brian Hanna

Theater of the Absurd

Some years ago a woman I admire put on a public reading of *A Man Born to be King* by Dorothy L. Sayers. She asked me if I would take the part of a Roman centurion. I said yes. I hadn't acted for many years, but it was a relatively minor role that I wouldn't even have to learn, because it was going to be read in a church by torchlight in the dark. The absence of illumination of course meant that scenery and costumes were not needed either, which my loyal wife said was just as well because a Roman centurion's tunic might reveal my spindly upper arms ("little chicken wings"), which prompted my son-in-law to loyally assert that I might actually have the legs for the outfit, if only one could see them in the dark.

Opening Night got under way. The actors were dotted around the church, their pale faces appropriately ghostly. In the darkness it seemed all was going well. In the last scene when Christ was on the Cross, Caiaphas the High Priest had just launched into his self-serving don't –blame- me- for- the- Crucifixion whine, when his reading light went out.

You can see the problem, can't you? Attempts to rush a back- up source of illumination to him were hampered by the fact that one couldn't find him in the dark. He, on the other hand, had to deal with the reality that the nearest surviving source of illumination belonged to an actress about twenty feet away across a stretch of pitch black audience, which contained a number of persons in wheelchairs unable to clear his path. It was like a stoner's pajama party during a power outage.

There remains a significant theological question as to why an all-powerful God would allow attempts to pay him homage to be sabotaged by the shortcomings of cut-price batteries (I dare not mention from where) or those tiny reading lights (available at the same location) that had been purchased for a dollar each; maybe He wanted to make a point about the perils of reliance on Chinese merchandize, but we don't have time to explore that fascinating issue now.

Nor do I intend in any way to diminish the Crucifixion, but I can testify that when Eric Idle sang, on a cross, in *The Life of Brian* (my name, you may recall. spooky coincidence?) "Always look on the bright side of Life," he seemed to be looking straight at me, so ever since I have felt in a way … called.

If there must be a beginning to my tale, I would have to say I was about twelve and already addicted to the laughter of classmates when my Victorian grandmother asked me what I wanted to do with my life.

I replied that I'd like to be an actor or a comedian. Granny, a Baptist teetotaler, wondered aloud whether I would be funny enough. Ignoring her invitation to feel insecure about the matter, I reminded her that that she had occasionally laughed at the great Scottish comedian Harry Lauder, although she claimed, "He was rather vulgar." Her lips pursed at the memory of just how vulgar he was. Then in a kinder vein, since she loved me and spoilt me rotten, she said that I would probably live a happier life being an amusing architect, like my father, or grandfather, than to "go on the Music Hall stage to entertain intoxicated smokers" and risk falling victim to "the wiles of all those bespangled female acrobats and contortionists."

Her advice prevailed but only just, since at the age of twelve the sleazy charms of bespangled female acrobats and contortionists were already starting to have a certain lurid appeal to me. But I discovered from one of her sisters that Granny had herself once ignored her own mother's sermonettes about the moral perils of show business when she married my handsome grandfather. She had met him when he was working his way through Architectural School by hiring village halls and with his glamorous sister at the piano singing, in a splendidly ringing tenor that I am told bore comparison with Jussi Bjorling's, such Victorian ballads, as "Come into the Garden, Maud." Maud just happened to be Granny's middle name. Spooky coincidence number two?

In my teens I became fascinated by the movies and the theater and continued to contemplate a life as an actor but soon figured that there was more to it than dressing up and swanning around the stage. To do it well like Marlon Brando it seems you had in some way to vacate your own self and invite another persona that you might not even like to inhabit your mind and body. It had to seem to be more than just play acting if it was to come off as real.

Two actors perhaps slightly envious of Laurence Harvey's popular success were lamenting a lack of discrimination in his choice of roles, his alleged frivolity and absence of serious principle, etc.... probably referring to persistent rumors that he was catting around on Margaret Leighton.

One actor said, "Give him a wig and he'll play Camille."

Another replied, "Ah, yes, perhaps . . . but not, I think, very well."

 I discovered before any real harm was done that I was a theatrical personality, rather than an actor. My heroes in that era were George Sanders and Clifton Webb, who to a degree seemed to suffer from the same deficiency as myself but had made careers out of it. They were supremely watchable and could toss off a line as if they had written it themselves.

But it wasn't just my limitations as an actor that undermined my will to continue; two events took place in quick succession that revealed the capability of the theater to humiliate you. They happened to other performers but at the risk of seeming monumentally self-referential, they occurred with such timeliness that I wondered if the universe may have been visiting upon on some luckless thespians catastrophic events mainly designed to make ME opt for a safer profession. I hate to think of these desperate entertainers being sacrificed merely to cause me have second thoughts.

The first instance was a Christmas pantomime. Pantomimes were Entertainments based loosely on well-known legends. Aladdin and Cinderella are cases in point. They are designed to appeal to the child in all of us (that is oblique-speak for a not-too-demanding Christmas audience). A pantomime is a sort of catch-all for a wide variety of acts that you don't see today like plate spinners and ventriloquists. .It also enabled actors "resting between engagements" as they whimsically call it, to have a couple of months of paid work.

The one of which I speak, "Robin Hood and his Merry Men," was a low-rent affair. Robin was in his forties, a small mouse-like man with a rather metallic singing voice and legs that did not fill out his ecru tights. Maid Marian, the ingénue, was in her forties too and although still handsome, her appearance was starting to suggest an open box of donuts in the Dressing Room.

Marian and Robin had to perform a specialty act consisting of a truncated version of the climax of "Swan Lake"--not a good choice for the tiny orchestral forces in the pit, and a particularly poor one for a diminutive hero and his ample amour. An attempt to hoist and hold her aloft resulted in his spindly legs twisting like overloaded steel columns before they collapsed, sending Maid Marian down into the orchestra pit butt first onto the timpani. The wretched

Robin peered nervously down into the pit to be rewarded with a volley of recriminations from Maid Marian. They looked and sounded for all the world like an old married couple.

This was bad enough, but what transpired a week or so later was even worse, showing what happens when an audience takes against a play and the performers.

In the '40s there had been a famous film comedy called "Kind Hearts and Coronets," principally remembered now for the virtuoso performance of Alec Guinness, who played eight or nine different characters, all members of the dotty Dascoyne family, one of whom had seduced and abandoned the mother of the hero played by Dennis Price, who sets out to avenge his late Mama and at the same time to inherit the Dascoyne title and the estates by murdering each family member that stood between him and his objective. Price, a perfectly good if somewhat mannered actor, was no match for the prodigious skills of Guinness. His career never fully recovered.

Some ten years later on the cusp of middle age he had been reduced to touring the provincial theaters, my hometown Belfast's among them. He arrived there at the head of a company, which was putting on one of that vast array of Agatha Christie style murder mysteries.

They are escapist fantasies often set in a large country house at a weekend party. There is a detective, an eccentric maid, and a snooty Butler--"Will there be anything else, Milady?--" a slightly vacuous leading man from a minor public school with no chin and a Bentley and an anyone-for-tennis accent, and finally of course one or more glamorous female victims. I have to confess I was not actually present during the debacle that follows, but the person who was is extremely reliable. He claims that the audience never seemed to become too involved with the play. Maybe the stately homes and weekend parties were outside their middle class preoccupations, or maybe they had had just one too many relatives in service in such establishments, or perhaps more likely just one too many in the Circle Bar after act two; but whatever the reason they were starting to heckle the performers.

Matters got out of hand when Price (playing the one with no chin and a Bentley) came upon the dead body of a young woman called Gwen that he supposedly had the hots for. She has been murdered in the library.

Distraught Price fell wailing upon the corpse, "Gwen. Oh Gwen, What shall I do?"

From the rear circle a male voice high pitched in a passable imitation of the victim but with an awesome clarity of diction shouted the fateful words: "OOOh. Have me while I'm still warm."

The cast struggled to the end but their hearts just weren't in it. I realized that I would be much too thin-skinned for that sort of thing.

I turned my attention to becoming an architect completing my studies in Oxford, and staying on as a lecturer in Design, which allowed me time to work for other people and eventually to go on my own. I got married and bought a three-story row house. It had an attic and was fifteen feet wide. It was renovated with student labor over one summer.

Our first problem stemmed from my new wife's fervent conviction that there were rats in the attic. I wasn't sure but I conceded that my hearing might have been compromised by listening to Bruckner.

I eventually agreed to call pest control. A figure arrived at the door that looked the spitting image of Peter Sellers in the role of the pedantic shop steward in "I am all right, Jack." He drove a white van, wore a spotless white uniform, had a canister with some sort of gas, a mask, and goggles. He also had a great many opinions, none of which contemplated any kind of doubt or uncertainty. At his instruction I cut a 2 'x 2' hole in the third floor ceiling while he drank tea and ate my chocolate biscuits, and, my wife later claimed, bored her behind off. Metaphorically of course.

I positioned a stepladder and held the bottom of it while this epitome of self-regard ascended through the hole I had cut for him.

There was a long pause, before he returned to earth. He was a changed man. "Oh Jesus, I nearly gassed a family of Pakis (short for Pakistanis) living in your roof space. They seemed to have spread across quite a few attics." He was right. My immediate neighbor, a bus driver from Karachi, had paid rent to the previous owner of my house and the owners of several other adjoining attics in our row for the use of their roof space to accommodate paying guests. My attic was an essential component to the growth of his Empire, being the gateway to all the others.

He was enraged when I announced my intention of locating our master bedroom there. He didn't give up easily, saying that I was taking away the homes of his extended family from a village back home in Pakistan, and was diminishing not only his income but also those of his neighbors, whose attics could only be reached through mine. He muttered darkly that his lawyer had told him that he had been operating long enough with the consent of the previous owners to have established Squatter's Rights, so he would therefore sue me for loss of income. I said that no mention of this encumbrance to my title had been made by the realtor or the previous owner. "You could try and sue them," he said, brightening.

Sounding as conciliatory as I could, I said that if he or preferably his lawyer brought me a sworn statement in writing outlining the precise length of time he had been operating his enterprise in my attic, as well as any legal licenses and approvals that governed the operation. I would study them and make a decision. I also demanded that his lawyer outline arguments in support of his assertion that squatter's rights had been established.

Within two hours a very nervous gentleman was on the phone saying that contrary to any impressions that might have been given, his client had never been in the enterprise of which we spoke and never intended to be so. He further hoped that since there wasn't really an issue that I would not feel it necessary to inform the authorities that our little misunderstanding had ever taken place, that of course he would immediately repair the party wall in which an opening seemed to have spontaneously occurred. I wished him no ill will and said that if any of his neighbors saw fit to accommodate his guests, that was up to them, but that I drew the line at a nightly procession of his countrymen at the end of my bed bound either for their mattress or his toilet. That was simply not on, but a bottle of excellent port would erase for now any memory that it had ever been contemplated; it was on my doorstep within the hour. Oddly enough, after this unpromising start we got on quite well, though never as well as both our sons did.

During construction I had help from my Irish brothers. Since one of them was taking Holy Orders, he was not minded to take secular ones, especially from his older brother. He wanted to spend all day taking nails out of old construction lumber that was headed for the fireplace anyway so I refused to pay for that. An experienced carpenter that I had hired to keep an eye on the students had been ready to work for a reduced rate if I provided the tools, but emboldened by apparent mutiny of the cleric- to-be he added his complaints about a saw I had provided. "Master Brian," he said in a West Country accent, "I tell you that there saw is so blunt that I could ride it bare-arsed to Banbury and back, and not even cut myself."

Banbury to Oxford and back would be about thirty miles, so I am prepared to stipulate that the saw HAD lost its edge.

The work was finally finished and I had a party for the crew, colleagues on the faculty of the School of Architecture, and a few potential clients. I was too broke to get real champagne, so I sought the advice of the amiable local pub owner, who owed me a small favor. He said that he had a lot of flagons of cider that had gone flat and a lot of empty champagne bottles with, he chortled at the perfection of our strategy, a recognizably impressive label still on them. He had supplied the bottles and their original contents to a college banquet. Together we put the cider into the champagne bottles and replaced the corks with a nifty little machine that he had borrowed. Before he replaced each cork he quickly added what he called his 'secret ingredient,' which produced a generous and authentic looking foam. A small sample revealed we had a tasty thirst quencher on our hands at effectively no cost. I could appear as a host of profligate generosity at no cost to myself, the fulfillment of a lifelong ambition.

The party went well: corks popped, bottles foamed, and plentiful quantities of our iced 'bubbly' flowed. It was pronounced to be particularly fine; numerous toasts to my skills as the architect of the renovation, and to my generosity as a host were ceremoniously quaffed. All was going swimmingly when my friend and co-creator of the champagne appeared rather nervously at the front door. Urged to come in, he replied hesitantly, "No, I won't come in but have you started the champagne?"

"Of course, it's almost finished," I boomed expansively. "Everybody loved it. Huge success." Lowering my voice to a confidential level, I whispered knowingly, "Obviously I won't share our little secret about what's in it."

"Probably that's best," said he. "Well, all's well then. Now I must be going. Have a great night."

He had barely left when my wife, who had been taking conducted tours, informed me there was a long queue forming outside our one bathroom, and we were running out of toilet paper.

The atmosphere deteriorated quickly; discipline and restraint from those queuing up evaporated and there was a mass exodus out to the small back garden, which had just been planted. After the party, everything there died and nothing subsequently grew.

The pub owner eventually confessed. There were two bottles of effervescent salts in his medicine cabinet, one a cold remedy, the other a laxative.

The bloody idiot must have used the wrong one.

Kelly McDowell

There Were a Dozen or so

The geese are acting strange,
ol' Margie said to me the other night
and explained how they tried to fly
but most of the time just paddled by
ol' McKinley's place by the RV park
next to the Welcome to Waldport sign, so
i got curious and took my kayak and had a paddle
between the pylons where they use to grow oysters,
someone told me once, and sure enough
there were a dozen or so;
mostly sleeping, but one who was staring off who knows
where,
so i paddled nearer and not a feather did i ruffle,
but when i got closer i smelled something floating in
from upwind from where my friends and i bobbed with the
tide
and following my nose found a dozen or so
elderly folk resting in the shade of their RV's
they waved, I waved, we all waved but one who took a toke
and said they fed the geese,
but I don't think that's why they stay.

Kelly McDowell

A Thought on Perspective

It sometimes gets so hot on the Oregon coast
it becomes a little history
'Back in 'oh three' it got up to ninety-five.

   Yes, sir,
those were dog days for fishing.'
Dad talked like that towards the end;
'Damndest cold I ever know'd,' he told me
one night after too much boxed wine, 'was
    in the Ardennes in '45 when it was so cold

        the trees
         exploded at night and we
thought it was artillery.'

and so it goes

and so it goes
a random thought
a bit of string undone by a breeze
a knot to seize and as I try
it becomes a random thought
a bit of string undone by
a random thought
and so it goes

Kelly McDowell

The Answer to the Question on Reincarnation

leaving Lewiston after ham and eggs
i drive toward Kamiah, Idaho
to fix my sister's leaky roof

at mile marker 117 a bearded man
                                    with a stop sign

                    bottle of water
yellow hardhat halts me in time for a monarch butterfly
new wings still unfurling
to dance its birth ballet on the hood of the car
ecstatic and joyful
i thought of my father who was neither
and wondered why one brought the thought of the other
until i arrived at my sister's
                                    heard the cries of loss
                    news of our father's suicide

Kelly McDowell

A Summer of Long Shadows (excerpt)

My siblings pour through the back door like a herd of lumberjack, and I know what will happen if I stay, so before she can protest I tell Mom I'm going to Hiroshi's and dart through the front door, grab my bike, and run as hard as I can, pushing the bike through the thick driveway gravel until I get to the road. Then I'm up, on and gone just as Danny and Henry scream for me to come back. "Mom wants you!"

I am already picking up speed, and laughing at them; that trick won't work, not anymore, and when I glance over my shoulder I see Henry flip me off.

I slap my butt, yell "kiss this," and ride on.

To get to Hiroshi's house, there's a long hill with a fast drop then a shorter one rising so quick if you go fast enough you can catch air at the top. Dad likes to do it in the pickup. As I shift through the gears, my legs begin to pedal so fast they look like car pistons and for a moment I'm riding the world's fastest bicycle; a lime-green metal flake Schwinn Stingray with a dark green banana seat, a five speed shifter, center-pull caliper brakes, high rise handle bars, a slick on the back, and a deluxe generator with front and rear lights. I got it for my ninth birthday. My cousin Sean bought it at the PX and had it shipped all the way from Vietnam along with a crossbow and a dagger made from human bone he got from a tribe in the mountains. Mom thinks the knife is disgusting. I think it's the coolest thing ever.

When I shift to fifth gear, the world becomes a blur with the bright March sun warm on my face and a breeze coming from a sky as blue as robin eggs. The hospital is a memory and I feel wonderful – whole – and it dawns on me that for the first time in my life I am not sick.

"Well, duh, doofus," I say out loud, and give out a long and loud war whoop until my throat reminds me it has stitches. No more pills, cough syrup, missed school – not that I minded, or having to go to the doctor, or spending days in bed, and the thought makes me so happy I stand on the pedals, let go of the handlebars, and sail down the road with my hands outstretched catching the wind.

Mrs. Heinmann, whose husband is the sheriff, is hoeing her flower garden and screams at me to "ride right or I'll tell your dad!" I just laugh and sail by.

It is impossible for me to go any faster when I hit the bottom of the hill, and when I go up the other side and hit the crest, cranking as hard as I can to keep up speed, my bike leaves the ground. I betcha I cleared a foot if I cleared an inch. I let go another war whoop which gets Mrs. McCann's old blind basset hound to howling, followed by Mrs. McCann, who yells for me to come and collect pop bottles later.

I slide around the corner, scattering gravel into the street, and now I can see Hiroshi's pointy head towering above the hedge. I start barking. There's a pause, then an answer, and it sounds like a pack of mutts. The barking started in second grade when Dad, after watching us chase a rabbit through Mrs. McCann's backyard, across our family's alfalfa field, and then down into Hell's Canyon where we lost it in the sagebrush, called us a pack of dogs.

I skid to a stop in front of the house and Hiroshi's sister, Miko, jumps up from where she is sitting and tries to run over to greet me, but the kimono she's wearing is so tight it's more of a shuffle-hop. She's finally able to grab my hand and won't let go even when I try to get off the bike. When she touches me, a wave of intense elation and joy fills me. In fact it makes me dizzy, then when Grace, Bill, Hiroshi, and his mother join us, and when they reach out and take hold, all their feelings collide in my head like rocks in a tin can. I get dizzy and confused and my nose begins to bleed. Not a trickle, like when Danny and I are boxing and he gets in a good jab, but like when Dad turns the irrigation water on in the spring and floods the fields. Miko shrieks, Bill turns pale, Grace looks away queasily, and Hiroshi, who tells me he's seen lots of bloody noses in Judo practice, tilts my head forward while Mrs. Nakamura takes a napkin from the table and presses it against my nose. It stops as quickly as it started and I explain it away as too much excitement, but it scares me. I wonder if this is what I'm going to have to deal with for the rest of my life. I wonder if Superman gets nose bleeds.

They'd been sitting beneath the cherry tree in the Nakamura's front lawn, and around a low table with blue tea pots, small red cups, and plates of desserts, when I arrive. There's a sprig of the cherry tree in a dark blue vase, and as I get off the bike, the wind picks up and showers the table with pink blossoms. It's beautiful and I am about to say something when Bill finally recovers enough to say something.

"You're alive!" Bill says, slugging me gently on the shoulder.

"I am," I say, and in Bill's touch I can tell he is happy to see me and sad to be who and what he is. I have to fight to keep the emotions down.

"Darn! I wanted your bike. When I heard you croaked, all I could imagine was that sweet ride." Tall and dark, Bill's the biggest, strongest kid in our school, and even the sixth graders know better than to pick on him.

He's tough. I guess having no mother and an alcoholic father makes you that way, but he and I have known each other since we were babies. We were the same height until last year when all of a sudden he shot up as tall as a corn stalk. Dad calls us Mutt and Jeff, and the girls call him all the time, especially Cindy Mann, the prettiest girl in the class, who asks if he needs help with homework: lucky cuss.

"Gee, I missed you too," I answer, slugging him back. He tells me I was the talk of the school last week and girls, including Miko, put notes on my desk. Miko immediately denies it and tries to kick him but is held back by Bill's hand on her forehead.

"Let go of me you...you..." Her little face is pinched in fury as she tries to hit him but her swings are hardly reaching halfway. Bill teases her for the pronunciation of her words, especially her 'L's' which come out as 'R's.' "I didn't put any note on William's desk."

"No, you put it inside his desk," Bill laughs. Miko's face is turning red with rage until Mrs. Nakamura comes to Bill's rescue and makes Miko stand quietly to the side pouting.

"And you missed the math test, lucky duck," Bill adds, then points to Hiroshi. "And he got the only 'A.'" Hiroshi smiles not-so-humbly and bows.

"We didn't think your mommy would let you come out and play so soon," Grace teases, and then hugs me. She missed me, she says, and asks if I am okay. I tell her I am crackerjack and mean it. When she touches me, I feel calm and steady. Grace is a rock, but there's worry too. Grace and I met in first grade when we got in a fight over a tether ball game and we've been friends since. Pretty and blond like her mom, Grace looks like a seventh grader, something my brothers and the rest of the boys have all noticed. But she takes no bull crap from anyone. Ask my brother Henry, who tried to get a feel at a neighbor's birthday party before Christmas and got a lap of ice cream and a beating by Dad for his efforts.

Hiroshi, who at first had crowded in with the rest, had gotten a discreet cough from his mother, and now stood back along with his sister. They waited until the right moment then bowed. They may drive a Chevy but Hiroshi's family is very traditional. His family moved here from Japan when he was in second grade, and I was the first kid he met. Mr. Nakamura, who buys lumber for a Japanese manufacturer, was one of the few Japanese officers to survive Iwo Jima, having been ordered not to kill himself by his commander. The World War Two vets at the VFW aren't too pleased he's here, especially Bill's dad who fought at Iwo Jima with the Marines, and I guess there's been notes on his car threatening to take revenge. Hiroshi has told me some his dad's war stories. They sound a lot like my dad's. But for Hiroshi and me it's comic books and Godzilla movies. His uncle is a big shot in Japanese movie making and worked on the Godzilla movies, so Hiroshi's got movie posters and Godzilla toys, and all in Japanese. It's pretty cool. From Hiroshi I've learned the world is a lot bigger than Lewiston, Idaho, and the word 'different' has no meaning unless I give it one.

I bow in return, and then everyone is bowing, including Mrs. Nakamura, so it looks like we're a bunch of those toy drinking birds bobbing their heads in glasses of water.

They want to see the stitches so I open my mouth so they can peer inside. Grace says they should have removed the vocal chords, Bill thinks they should have added another brain or at least transplanted the defective one, and Hiroshi, giggling like his sister, asks to let him cut the stitches out with his dad's Samurai sword.

Miko, feeling left out, grabs the front of my shirt, pulls me down to her level, pinches me on the arm and in a stream of words that show no sign of stopping, tells me how scared she was when she heard I was in the hospital, and cried when someone at school said I was already dead… She starts to cry a little, then wiping the tears on her sleeve and taking a breath, continues by complaining how no one would tell her anything, no one would let her call my family or anything, and because of me, her black-as-coal eyes darting angrily towards her mother, she would now have to pay for the joss sticks she used praying for me out of her allowance. I ask her how many joss sticks she burned and she is telling me when she stops mid-sentence and stares into my eyes a moment likes she's found something unexpected. Her little pixie face, framed in her page boy haircut, is so serious I begin to laugh. She pokes me in the chest.

"You're not the same are you?" Not waiting for my answer she turns to her brother and tells him I'm not the same, does the same thing to her mom, only now there's a little fear in it. She clamps her hands on my head and getting so close our noses are nearly touching, peers deeper, then shaking her head as if she's already made up her mind, says "You're not the same."

It was matter-of-fact and it was the truth, and as much as I wanted to tell her I was a freak, I see ghosts, and when people touch me I know their feelings and all their secrets, I was afraid what Grandpa said would come true. *You'll be a Judas goat if they know, lad, so keep the secret close. Keep it safe.*

I lie. "Of course not, dork," I say, grabbing her cheeks and pinching them. "I have no tonsils. Duh!" She pinches me back, harder, and says that's not what she meant.

"Perhaps William-san would like some tea?" Mrs. Nakamura interrupts. Taking her daughter's hand, they lead us to a small table where I have my first Cherry Blossom Festival. Years later, when I was stationed in Japan in the Navy, Hiroshi, Miko, and their families would share another festival with me – in Kyoto. Miko and her daughter were wearing the same kimonos.

Marguerite K.A. Petersen

Widowed

I pace my back porch
like a widow's walk of old
back and forth, back and forth
watching and waiting for you
who will never return

I feel your presence
and memories flood in
the surf rolls inexorably on
drowning my tears

Marguerite K.A. Petersen

Treasure

you knew more of me
than anyone on this planet
you were my best friend

others know only facets of me
you knew the whole gem
as you called me min skat*
my treasure

*skat: From Old Norse: treasure

Marguerite K.A. Petersen

The Quiet Times

I miss the quiet times
the most
when you were reading in your study
and I in mine working on my computer.
We enjoyed the companionable silence.
Now and then you would say, "Here's something
you might be interested in," and you'd read
me a few paragraphs. You were always right.

Or when the children and grandchildren
left after a hectic visit. We'd stand
on the front porch, your arm around my shoulders
and sigh. "It's nice to be just the two of us,"
you'd say and I would agree.

Or when we'd watch a movie together in the evening.
No words were needed. We knew what the other enjoyed.

Now the quiet times are the worst.
The silence stretches.

Authors

Brian Hanna was born in Ireland. From the time he was a toddler he enjoyed playing with words. "We were too poor to buy toys, but words are cheap," he explains. He considered careers in law and on the stage but abandoned the law on discovering it wasn't just about eloquence and swanning around in a wig. Stage ambitions were, he admits, quickly abandoned for precisely the same reasons. For most of his working life he has been an architect in Canada. Now he mostly writes comedy pieces. It doesn't make any money, but it doesn't cost that much either. The outlays on writing seminars and self-publishing are, he imagines, modest, when compared to the costs of keeping a mistress or a time share in the Virgin Islands.

Ruth F. Harrison is a retired professor of medieval literature. Publications include two textbooks, five poetry collections (*Bone Flute*, 1996; *Namesong*, 2004; *How Singular and Fine*, a collection of formal poetry, 2012; *West of 101*, 2013; *among the cat tales*, 2014; three chapbooks; poems included in Turco's *The Book of Forms* (2012) and in *The Lyric*'s children's anthology (2012). Her recent work appears in *Harp Strings, Kestrel, Denver Quarterly, Plainsong, The Lyric, Trinacria,* and many other journals, and in the Oregon bridges anthology; and online in *packratnesi* and Lewis Turco's blog. Her poems have won numerous awards in *Formalist*, NFSPS, and OPA (OSPA) contests. She has been awarded a lifetime membership in OPA.

Sandra Mason's full-length poetry collection, *Lost and Found*, was just released in late 2014. Her earlier collection, *Poems Along the Way*, is a reworking of poems of the Chinese masters. A late bloomer, now in retirement from a life-long career in academics, she finally has time to write and is working on memoirs, a novella, and film noir.

Kelly McDowell moved to the Oregon coast last year from Idaho, where he taught 6th grade. A retired U.S. Navy Sonarman, he spent his military career surfing and hunting Russian submarines - in that order. After his retirement he fixed copiers, worked as a reporter for the *Malheur Enterprise* in Vale, Oregon, finished a master's degree, and re-discovered his love for writing fiction. He is working on his first novel, *A Summer of Long Shadows,* a series of short stories, and poetry…poor as it might be. He lives along the Alsea River.

Sue McGhee lives in Colorado most of the year, with annual visits to the central Oregon coast. She is currently working on her memoirs as well as a sequel to her first novel, *When the Eagles Fly with the Condor*, published in 2011.

Marguerite K. A. Petersen (known as Marg) has been writing poetry since she was 16 when she got locked out of her house and got bored so she sat down on the steps and wrote a sonnet to a tree. She lived in Corvallis for 33 years before moving to Yachats in 2001 with her husband, Bent. She has been in several poetry groups and worked as a secretary at several places mainly at peak.org.

Shirley Plummer's recent experience has prompted reassessment and reconsideration of life, purpose, direction, goals. It is a kind of death and rebirth with a blank slate – an opportunity to reformulate my self, my poetic thrust – and I proceed cautiously to determine what should be entered on the slate. I mean to couple with caution the abandon and curiosity of the infant.

Patricia Ranzoni's work has been published across the country and abroad, including previous issues of the TUESDAY anthology, having participated with the group for a decade. Home is with family on the Maine and

Oregon coasts. In 2013 she was nominated for a St. Botolph Foundation Emerging Artist Award. Her ninth book, *FLIGHTS & GLORIES, Poems Between the Atlantic & Pacific,* will be published by Turnstone Books of Oregon, and this past year she became Poet Laureate for life of Bucksport, Maine.